THIS WALKER BOOK BELONGS TO:

Kate M

For Patrick and Ben
(the noisiest and best!)

ACKNOWLEDGEMENTS

The publisher gratefully acknowledges permission to use the following material:

On the Ning Nang Nong © Spike Milligan, from *Silly Verse for Kids*, published by Puffin Books. **Ears Hear**, Hymes Jr, from *Oodles of Noodles* © Lucia and James L. Hymes Jr, reprinted by permission of Addison Wesley Publishing Company, Inc. **Laughing Time** © 1990 William Jay Smith, reprinted from *Laughing Time: Collected Nonsense*, by permission of Farrar, Strauss & Giroux, Inc. **Commissariat Camels**, reprinted by permission of A. P. Watt Ltd on behalf of The National Trust for Places of Historic Interest or Natural Beauty. **"Quack!" said the Billy Goat** © Charles Causley, from *Figgie Hobbin*, published by Pan Macmillan. **Quack, Quack!** © 1979 Dr Seuss Enterprises, L P, from *Oh, Say, Can You Say?*, reprinted by permission of Random House, Inc. **Early Walkman**, **Kitchen Sink – Song** and **City Music** © Tony Mitton, reprinted by permission of Murray Pollinger Literary Agent. **Our Washing Machine** © 1963, 1991 Patricia Hubbell, reprinted by permission of Marian Reiner for the author. **The Small Ghostie** © Barbara Ireson, from *Rhyme Time*, published by Hamlyn. **Steel Band Jump Up** © Faustin Charles, reprinted by permission of M. C. Martinez Literary Agency. **Fishes' Evening Song** © 1967 Dahlov Ipcar, reprinted by permission of McIntosh & Otis, Inc. **The Sound Collector** © Roger McGough, from *Pillow Talk*, published by Viking, reprinted by permission of Peters, Fraser & Dunlop.

First published 1997 by Walker Books Ltd
87 Vauxhall Walk, London SE11 5HJ

This edition published 1999

2 4 6 8 10 9 7 5 3 1

Illustrations © 1997 Debi Gliori

This book has been typeset in Cafeteria.

Printed in Hong Kong

British Library Cataloguing in Publication Data
A catalogue record for this book is
available from the British Library.

ISBN 0-7445-6751-3 (hb)
ISBN 0-7445-6996-6 (pb)

Noisy Poems

Illustrated by
Debi Gliori

WALKER BOOKS
AND SUBSIDIARIES
LONDON • BOSTON • SYDNEY

Ears Hear

Flies buzz,
Motors roar.
Kettles hiss,
People snore.
Dogs bark,
Birds cheep.
Autos honk: *Beep! Beep!*

Winds sigh,
Shoes squeak.
Trucks honk,
Floors creak.
Whistles toot,
Bells clang.
Doors slam: *Bang! Bang!*

Kids shout,
Clocks ding.
Babies cry,
Phones ring.
Balls bounce,
Spoons drop.
People scream: *Stop! Stop!*

Lucia and James L. Hymes Jr

BUZZZZzzzz

toot!

CLANG!

woof!

creak!

SQUEA

Laughing Time

It was laughing time, and the tall Giraffe
Lifted his head, and began to laugh:
Ha! Ha! Ha! Ha!

Ha!
Ha!
Ha!
Ha!

And the Chimpanzee on the ginkgo tree
Swung merrily down with a Tee Hee Hee:
Hee! Hee! Hee! Hee!

Tee Hee Hee
Hee! Hee! Hee!

"It's certainly not against the law!"
Croaked Justice Crow with a loud guffaw:
Haw! Haw! Haw! Haw!

Haw! Haw! Haw! Haw!

The dancing Bear who could never say "No"
Waltzed up and down on the tip of his toe:
Ho! Ho! Ho! Ho!

The Donkey daintily took his paw,
And around they went:
Hee-haw! Hee-haw! Hee-haw! Hee-haw!

The Moon had to smile as it started to climb;
All over the world it was laughing time!
Ho! Ho! Ho! Ho! Hee-haw! Hee-haw!
Hee! Hee! Hee! Hee! Ha! Ha! Ha! Ha!

William Jay Smith

Quack, Quack!

We have two ducks. One blue. One black.
And when our blue duck goes "Quack-quack"
our black duck quickly quack-quacks back.
The quacks Blue quacks make her quite a quacker
but Black is a quicker quacker-backer.

Dr Seuss

Commissariat Camels

We haven't a camelty tune of our own
To help us trollop along.
But every neck is a hairy trombone,
Rtt-ta-ta-ta! is a hairy trombone.
And this is our marching song:
Can't! Don't! Shan't! Won't!
Pass it along the line!

Rudyard Kipling

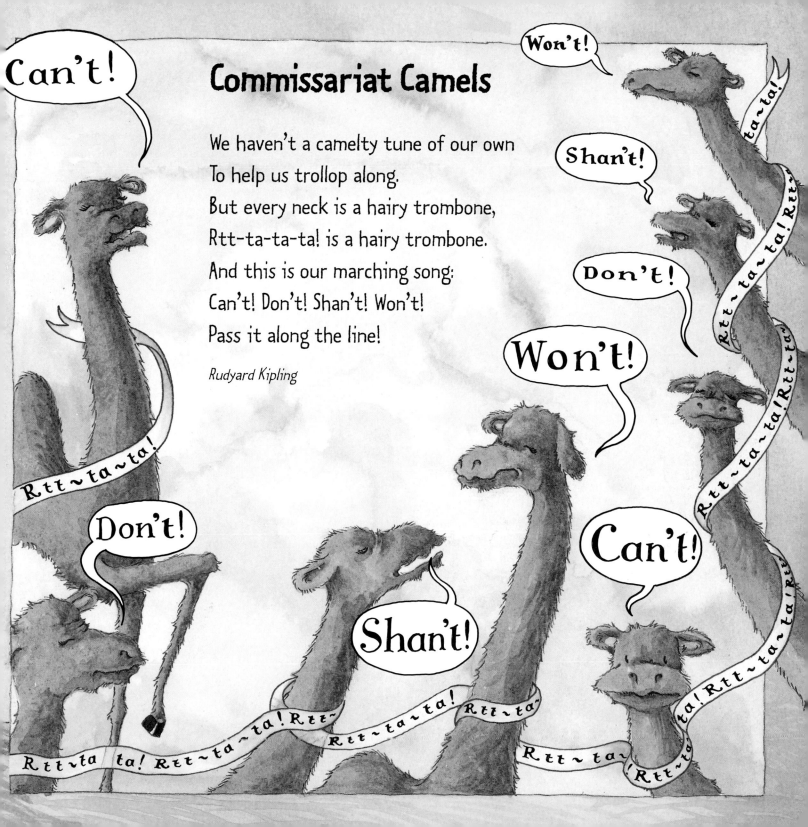

"Quack!" Said the Billy Goat

"Quack!" said the billy goat,
   "Oink!" said the hen.
"Miaow!" said the little chick
   Running in the pen.

"Hobble-gobble!" said the dog,
   "Cluck!" said the sow.
"Tu-whit-tu-whoo!" the donkey said,
   "Baa!" said the cow.

"Hee-haw!" the turkey cried,
  The duck began to moo.
All at once the sheep went,
  "Cock-a-doodle-doo!"
"Bleat! Bleat!" said the owl
  When he began to speak.
"Bow-wow!" said the cock
  Swimming in the creek.

"Cheep-cheep!" said the cat
  As she began to fly.
"Farmer's been and laid an egg –
  That's the reason why."

Charles Causley

Kitchen Sink-Song

Tap goes drip-drip
plip-plip-plink.
Tap goes trickle at the
kitchen sink.
Fridge goes gurgle
Pan goes slop.
Bin goes flip-flap
Toast goes POP!

Tony Mitton

Our Washing Machine

Our washing machine went whisity whirr
Whisity whisity whisity whirr
One day at noon it went whisity click
Whisity whisity whisity click
Click grr click grr click grr click
Call the repairman
Fix it ... Quick!

Patricia Hubbell

The Small Ghostie

When it's late and it's dark
And everyone sleeps . . . shhh shhh shhh,
Into our kitchen
A small ghostie creeps . . . shhh shhh shhh.

We hear knocking and raps
And then rattles and taps,

Then he clatters and clangs
And he batters and bangs,

And he whistles and yowls
And he screeches and howls . . .

So we pull up our covers over our heads
And we block up our ears and
WE STAY IN OUR BEDS.

Barbara Ireson

Auntie's Skirts

Whenever Auntie moves around
Her dresses make a curious sound;
They trail behind her up the floor,
And trundle after through the door.

Robert Louis Stevenson

New Shoes

My shoes are new and squeaky shoes,
They're very shiny, creaky shoes,
I wish I had my leaky shoes
That Mummy threw away.

I liked my old brown leaky shoes
Much better than these creaky shoes,
These shiny, creaky, squeaky shoes
I've got to wear today.

Anonymous

squeak

creak

Early in the Morning

Come down to the station early in the morning,
See all the railway trains standing in a row.
See all the drivers starting up the engines,
Clickety click and clackety clack,
Off they go!

Come down to the garage early in the morning,
See all the buses standing in a row.
See all the drivers starting up the engines,
Rumble, rumble, rumble, rumble,
Off they go!

Whirr

Whirr

Clickety click clackety clack

Rumble

Rumble

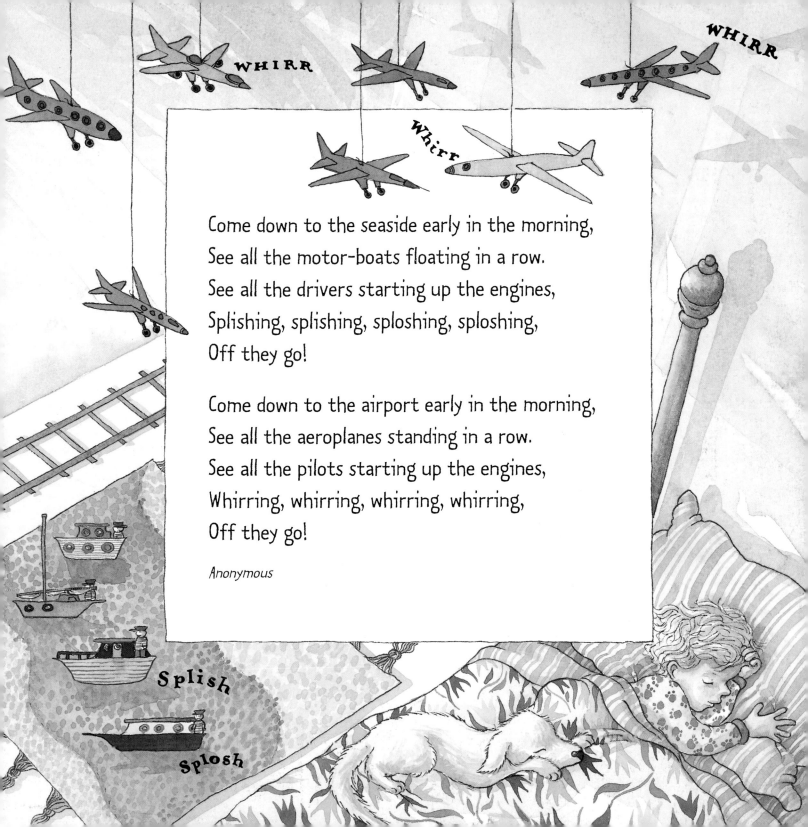

WHIRR

WHIRR

Whirr

Come down to the seaside early in the morning,
See all the motor-boats floating in a row.
See all the drivers starting up the engines,
Splishing, splishing, sploshing, sploshing,
Off they go!

Come down to the airport early in the morning,
See all the aeroplanes standing in a row.
See all the pilots starting up the engines,
Whirring, whirring, whirring, whirring,
Off they go!

Anonymous

Splish

Splosh

Steel Band Jump Up

I put my ear to the ground,
And I hear the steel-band sound:
Ping pong! Ping pong!
Music deep, rhythm sweet,
I'm dancing tracking the beat;
Like a seashell's ringing song,
Ping pong! Ping pong!
Moving along, moving along,
High and low, up and down,
Ping pong! Ping pong!
Pan beating singing, round and round,
Ping pong! Ping pong!

Faustin Charles

City Music

Snap your fingers.
Tap your feet.
Step out a rhythm
down the street.

Rap on a litter bin.
Stamp on the ground.
City music
is all around.

Beep says motor-car.
Ding says bike.
*City music
is what we like.*

Tony Mitton

Early Walkman
(5 million years ago)

Fasten sea-shell
on to each ear.
Listen. Amazing!
What me hear?

Sound of water,
wind and rain
washing about
inside my brain.

Stand on two legs.
Walk along.
Listening to
that sea-shell song.

Tony Mitton

Fishes' Evening Song

Flip flop,
Flip flap,
Slip slap,
Lip lap;
Water sounds,
Soothing sounds.

We fan our fins
As we lie
Resting here
Eye to eye.
Water falls
Drop by drop

Plip plop,
Drip drop.
Plink plunk,
Splash splish;
Fish fins fan,
Fish tails swish,

Swush, swash, swish.
This we wish . . .
Water cold,
Water clear,
Water smooth,
Just to soothe
Sleepy fish.

Dahlov Ipcar

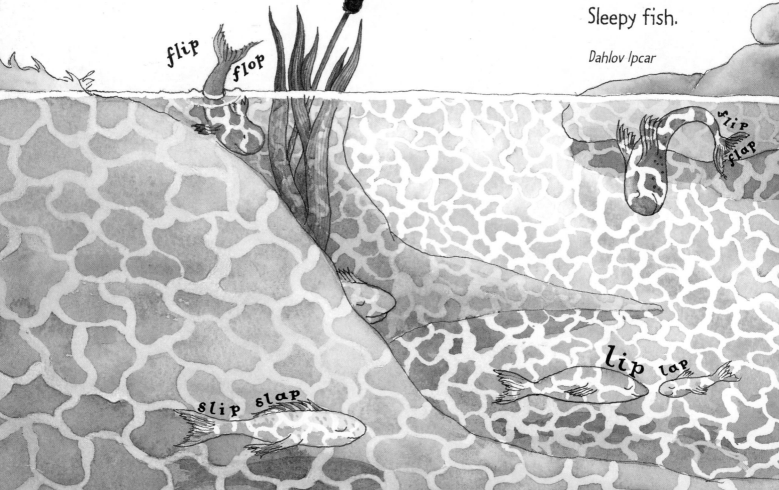

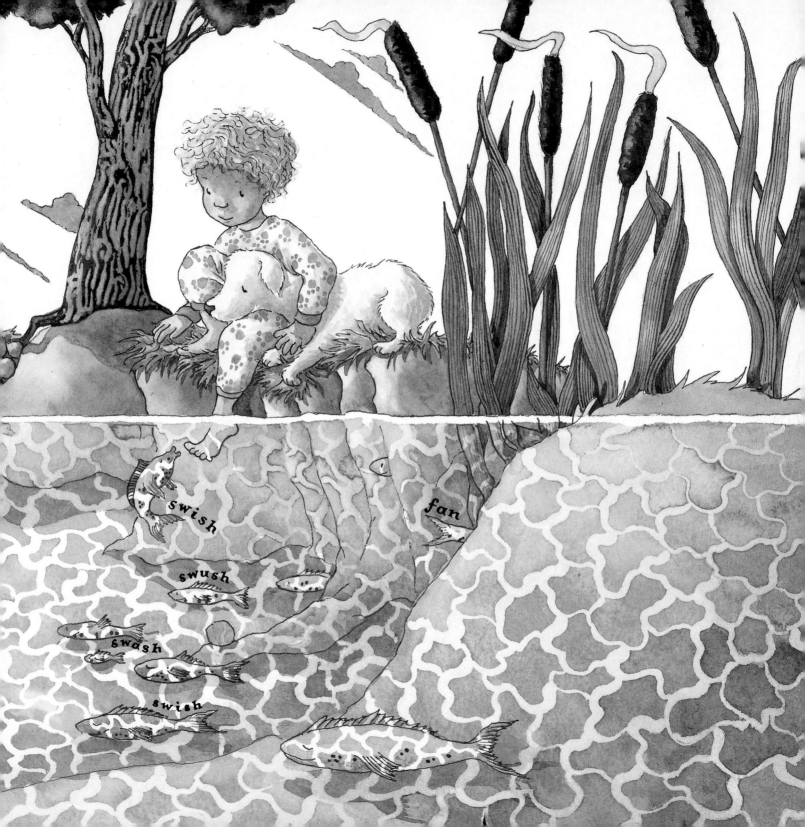

The Sound Collector

A stranger called this morning
Dressed all in black and grey
Put every sound into a bag
And carried them away

The whistling of the kettle
The turning of the lock
The purring of the kitten
The ticking of the clock

The popping of the toaster
The crunching of the flakes
When you spread the marmalade
The scraping noise it makes

The hissing of the frying-pan
The ticking of the grill
The bubbling of the bathtub
When it starts to fill

The drumming of the raindrops
On the window-pane
When you do the washing-up
The gurgle of the drain

The crying of the baby
The squeaking of the chair
The swishing of the curtain
The creaking of the stair

A stranger called this morning
He didn't leave his name
Left us only silence
Life will never be the same.

Roger McGough

MORE WALKER PAPERBACKS
For You to Enjoy

A CUP OF STARSHINE
compiled by Jill Bennett, illustrated by Graham Percy

In this lively anthology for young children you'll find poems about subjects as diverse as washing and springtime, playing and the moon…

"A beautifully produced and illustrated anthology." *Independent on Sunday*

0-7445-6097-7   £6.99

ASANA AND THE ANIMALS
by Grace Nichols/Sarah Adams

This book sings with the rhymes of a little girl called Asana, who celebrates the animals that she knows and likes and dreams about – from a caterpillar to a Jersey cow, a hedgehog to a jogging ocelot, a giraffe to her grandmother's cat!

"All the poems read aloud well and will prompt lively discussion." *The School Librarian*

0-7445-5498-5   £5.99

OUT AND ABOUT
by Shirley Hughes

Eighteen richly illustrated poems portray the weather and activities associated with the various seasons.

"Hughes at her best. Simple, evocative rhymes conjure up images that then explode in the magnificent richness of her paintings." *The Guardian*

0-7445-6062-4   £6.99

Walker Paperbacks are available from most booksellers, or by post from B.B.C.S., P.O. Box 941, Hull, North Humberside HU1 3YQ
24 hour telephone credit card line 01482 224626

To order, send: Title, author, ISBN number and price for each book ordered, your full name and address, cheque or postal order payable to BBCS for the total amount and allow the following for postage and packing:
UK and BFPO: £1.00 for the first book, and 50p for each additional book to a maximum of £3.50.
Overseas and Eire: £2.00 for the first book, £1.00 for the second and 50p for each additional book.

Prices and availability are subject to change without notice.